PICTURES

..OF...

KNOXVILLE

A Reproduction by Charles A. Reeves, Jr.
Original published ca 1904.

Charles A. Reeves, Jr.
Technical Illustration & Publishing
Specializing in Cartography and Genealogy

10812 Dineen Drive   (865) 966-5768
Knoxville, Tennessee 37934-1809
e-mail: reevesca@tds.net
Home Page: http://ReevesMaps.com

ISBN 978-0-9800984-3-3

How this booklet was produced: Charles' original copy was scanned at 300 dpi and the images edited in Adobe Photoshop to remove artifacts. The pages were scanned in color, although the original photographs were black-and-white. They were then converted to greyscale for this printing.

Note: The original format of this booklet was horizontal. Because of printing limiations, the format for this version has been revised to vertical, requiring some editorial changes from the original. However, in the editor's opinion at least, the end result is that it is much easier to read.

KNOXVILLE

Verily some people seem to be born lucky — and it is so with communities as with individuals. But it is claimed by some that it is better to be born poor than rich, and the reasons given will again apply to communities as well as to individuals. By way of illustrating the latter point, let us take the State of Massachusetts. The Puritans landed on a rock, and later on found that Massachusetts was pretty much all rock. Barren prospects developed the resourceful Yankee, and the old Bay State became covered with manufacturing plants where were assembled all the products of more favored states and made up into articles which we must have — and the descendants of the old Puritans waxed rich.

When the Creator completed this earth for its people He pigeon-holed a lot of gilt-edged securities in that section now embraced by some thirty counties of East Tennessee, put on a time lock, and Knoxville's destiny was to find the combination, open the vault and disclose the treasures. When in need of anything she leisurely removed a portion of the treasury, sent it to the aforesaid Yankee for a consideration, which supplied present needs, and she got along comfortably, to be sure!

And what were those treasures? Chiefly they were COAL, IRON, TIMBER, MARBLE, COPPER, ZINC, BARYTA, LEAD, SLATE, and a long list of other minerals, located in scores of places undeveloped because inaccessible. The Yankee took these things and converted them into other shapes, such as furniture, agricultural implements, tools of all sorts, steel bridges, etc., and convinced us of the necessity of them, and we took them at their prices!

A combination of events, such as war's desolations, advent of railroads, a baptism of commercial enterprise, aroused pride, and a quickened appreciation of environment and opportunity caused Knoxville, which had grown to importance in spite of herself, to shake off her moss and become a giant of the mountains in truth and a leader in southern progress. In the exercise of her new strength and activity she is reaching out and taking some of those Yankees by the scruffs of their necks and bringing them and their factories to her territory and making them her willing subjects. Old Massachusetts herself has contributed to Knoxville next to the largest cotton mill in the South.

Her practically inexhaustible treasury of raw products is being increasingly drawn upon, and the proportion manufactured at home is correspondingly growing. Some fifteen factories ship their furniture to all portions of the globe. The same may be said of our oak extract, cotton, marble, and woolen products; and our manufactured iron has a growing trade in twenty-one states. Our wagons and carriages, brick, tinware, trunks and bags, suspenders, soap, coffins, clothing and knit goods of all kinds, paper and pine boxes, bed canopies, coke and by-products, fertilizers, flour and meal, warm air furnaces, iron and brass foundry products, photo-engraving, distilled products (of course), patent medicines, cars of all kinds, carbonated drinks, confectionery, cigars, chewing gum, bakers' products, mattresses, beer, steam boilers, and so on, work territories of from six to twenty-four states.

In short, Knoxville is the metropolis and center of the division of East Tennessee, and possesses these advantages: Two of the largest and strongest competing railway systems of the South, the Louisville & Nashville and the Southern, and their branches which permeate our mountains of timber and minerals and our valleys of fruit, stock and agricultural products.

A navigable river which, with twelve other rivers and mountain streams, furnishes a system of transportation to her door which supplements the railroads and holds excessive freight rates in check.

The third largest jobbing trade in the South.

The University of Tennessee and the Summer School of the South.

A superb public school system and a number of private institutes of art and learning.

Nearly 200 miles of pike roads leading out of the city.

Absolutely no better and purer water is furnished any city.

A fine street car system.

Churches of every denomination — nearly.

An altitude of 1,000 feet above sea level.

An all-year-round climate for labor.

A health-giving atmosphere, loaded with mountain freshness and ozone.

About 60,000 of as hospitable people as you can find on the globe.

GAY STREET, INTERSECTION OF CLINCH AVENUE, ON A BUSY DAY.

GAY STREET, NORTH OF DEPOT AVENUE.

GAY STREET, SOUTH OF MAIN AVENUE.

DEPOT AVENUE EAST OF GAY STREET, SHOWING SOUTHERN
RAILWAY STATION.

VINE AVENUE, EAST OF GAY STREET.

4

WALL AVENUE, WEST OF GAY STREET.

UNION AVENUE, WEST OF GAY STREET.

CLINCH AVENUE, WEST OF GAY STREET.

CHURCH AVENUE, WEST OF GAY STREET.

PRINCE STREET.
Showing Post Office and Custom House and the Empire and Deaderick Office Buildings.

GAY STREET JOBBING HOUSES, NORTH FROM GAUT-OGDEN CO.

WEST HILL AVENUE.

WEST MAIN AVENUE.

GROUP OF CITY BRIDGES.

9

HIGHLAND AVENUE.

WEST CLINCH AVENUE

LAUREL AVENUE.

NORTH FOURTH AVENUE.

NORTH FIFTH AVENUE.

WASHINGTON AVENUE.

K. E. CO.

GROUP OF CHARITABLE INSTITUTIONS.

INTERIOR LAWSON-McGHEE FREE LIBRARY.

WOMAN'S BUILDING.
Home of Knoxville Women's Clubs and the Knoxville Chamber of Commerce.

IN THE UNIVERSITY OF TENNESSEE GROUNDS.

SECTIONAL VIEW UNIVERSITY OF TENNESSEE FARM AND AGRICULTURAL EXPERIMENT STATION.

IN THE GROUNDS OF THE UNIVERSITY OF TENNESSEE, SUMMER SCHOOL OF THE SOUTH, JUNE, 1903.

BAKER-HIMEL RESIDENCE.

BAKER-HIMEL SCHOOL.
Knoxville's Boarding and Day School for Boys.

16

TENNESSEE DEAF AND DUMB SCHOOL.

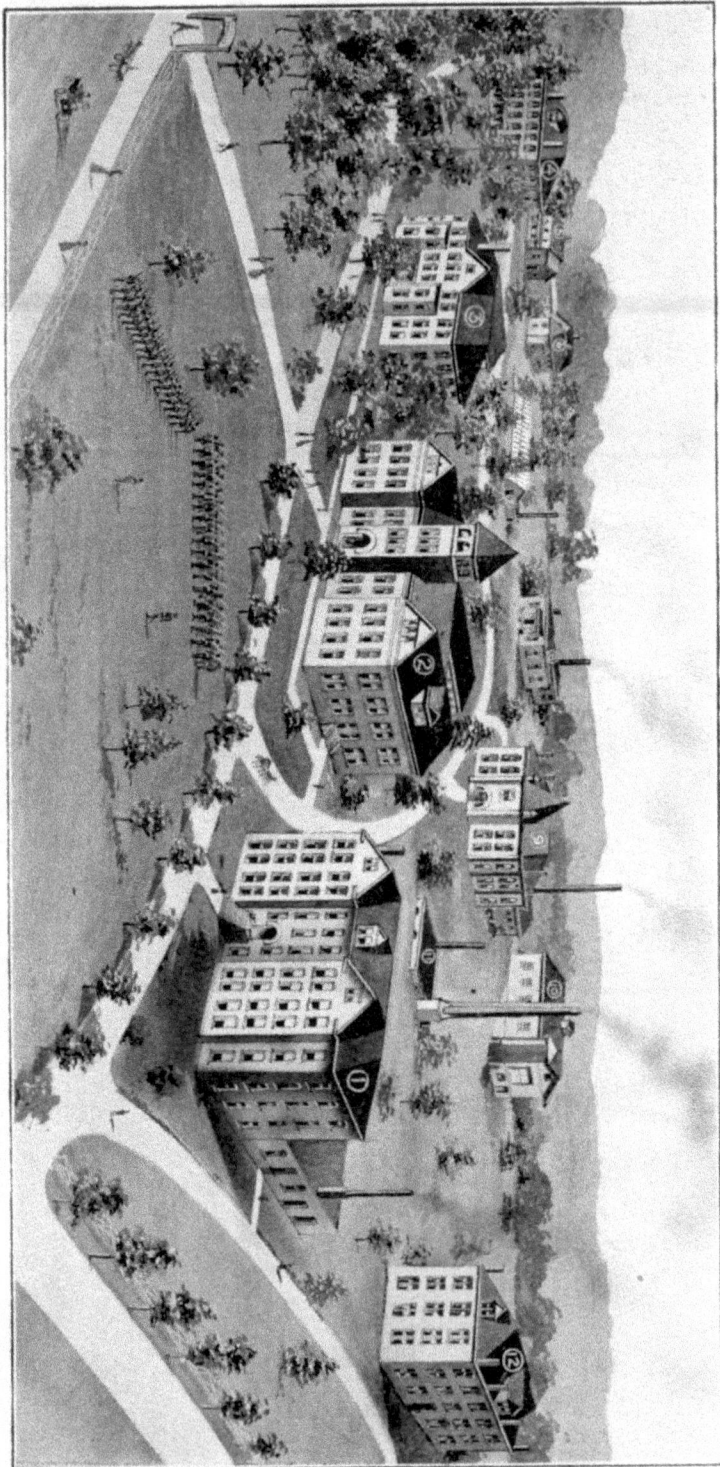

KNOXVILLE COLLEGE—LEADING INSTITUTION IN EAST TENNESSEE FOR COLORED YOUTH.

1. Elnathan Hall, for young women.
2. Recitation Hall.
3. McCulloch Hall, for young men.
4. Wallace Hall—Teachers' Home and Literary Society Halls.
5. Professor's Residence.
6. President's House.
7. Greenhouse.
8. Dairy Building.
9. Mechanical Building.
10. Barn, with silo.
11. Heating Plant.
12. McDill Home, for girls.

"WOODSIDE," ONE OF THE NEW BUILDINGS OF THE EASTERN HOSPITAL FOR INSANE AT LYON'S VIEW.

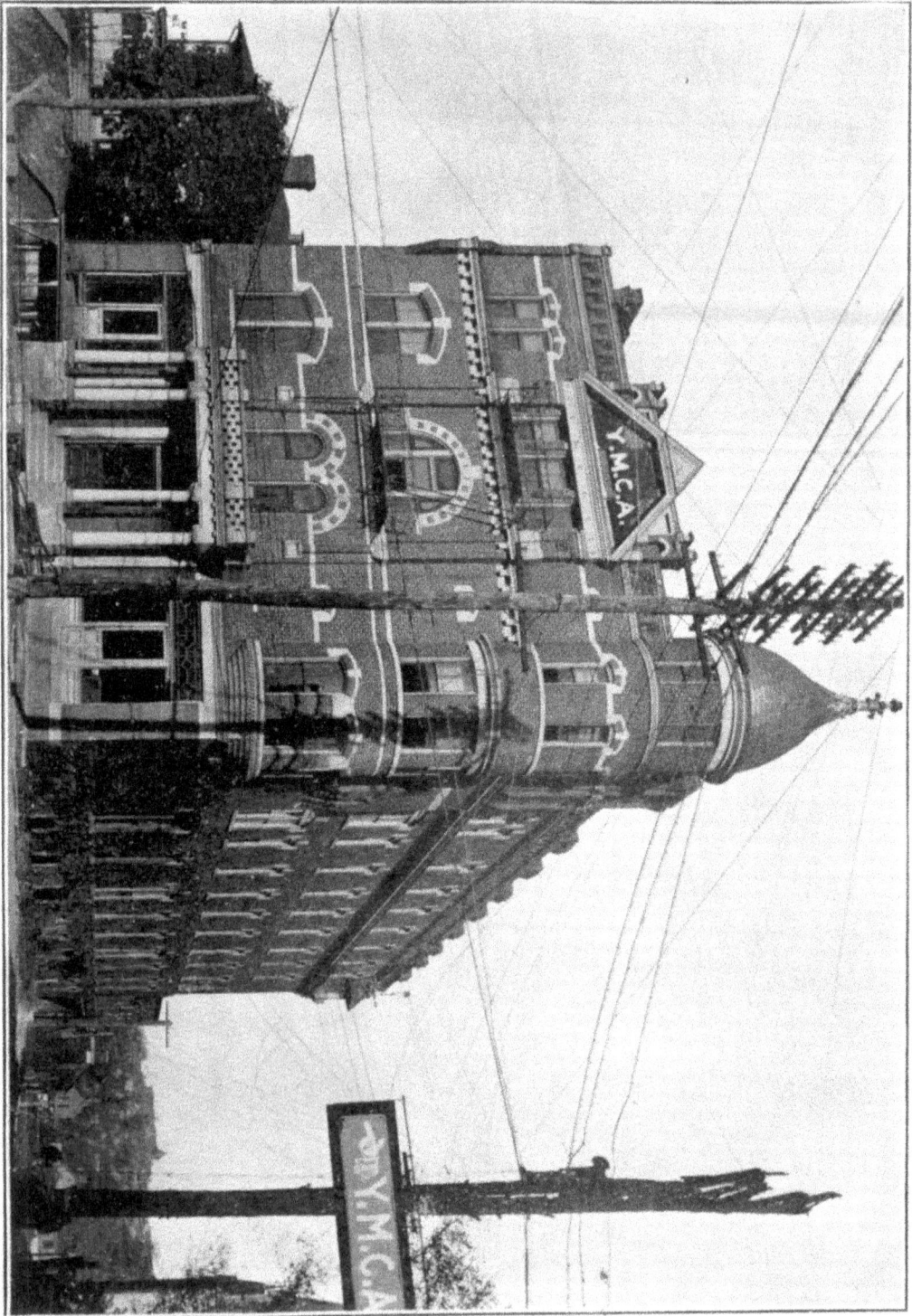

NEW BUILDING, CENTRAL Y. M. C. A. CORNER COMMERCE AVENUE AND STATE STREET.

THE JOURNAL AND TRIBUNE.

VOLUME XVII., NO. 104.   KNOXVILLE, TENN., TUESDAY MORNING, AUGUST 4, 1903   Price Daily 2c., On Trains and Sunday, 5c

BROADWAY AND KINGSTON PIKES.

MARYVILLE PIKE.

WOODLAWN PIKE.

SEVIERVILLE PIKE.

INTAKE TOWER AT KNOXVILLE WATER COMPANY'S MAIN PUMPING STATION.
Using the Latest Invention of William Wheeler, Boston.

INTERIOR FILTER PLANT, KNOXVILLE WATER COMPANY,
Showing the Warren Filter, furnished by the Cumberland Manufacturing Company, Boston, Mass.

FILTERING PLANT, KNOXVILLE WATER COMPANY.
105 feet high-pressure Stand Pipe giving the city 90 pounds pressure.

KNOX COUNTY COURT HOUSE.

PILGRIM CONGREGATIONAL CHURCH.

ST. JONH'S EPISCOPAL, CHURCH.

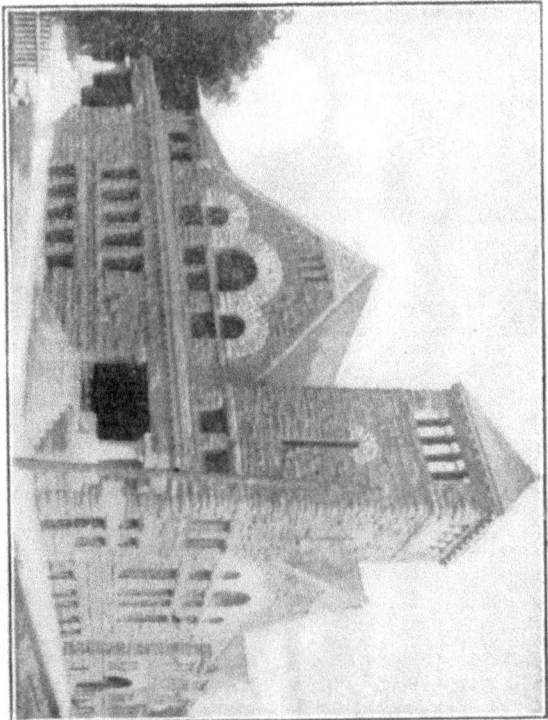

FIRST PRESBYTERIAN CHURCH.

FIRST M. E. CHURCH.

CHURCH STREET M. E. CHURCH, SOUTH.

FIRST BAPTIST CHURCH.

SECOND PRESBYTERIAN CHURCH.

CHURCH OF THE IMMACULATE CONCEPTION.
(Catholic.)

Library.   Dining Room.   Sitting Room.

RESIDENCE OF MR. GEORGE W. CALLAHAN, AT DANTE.

FARM RESIDENCE OF MR. GEORGE W. CALLAHAN, AT DANTE, FIVE MILES NORTH OF KNOXVILLE.

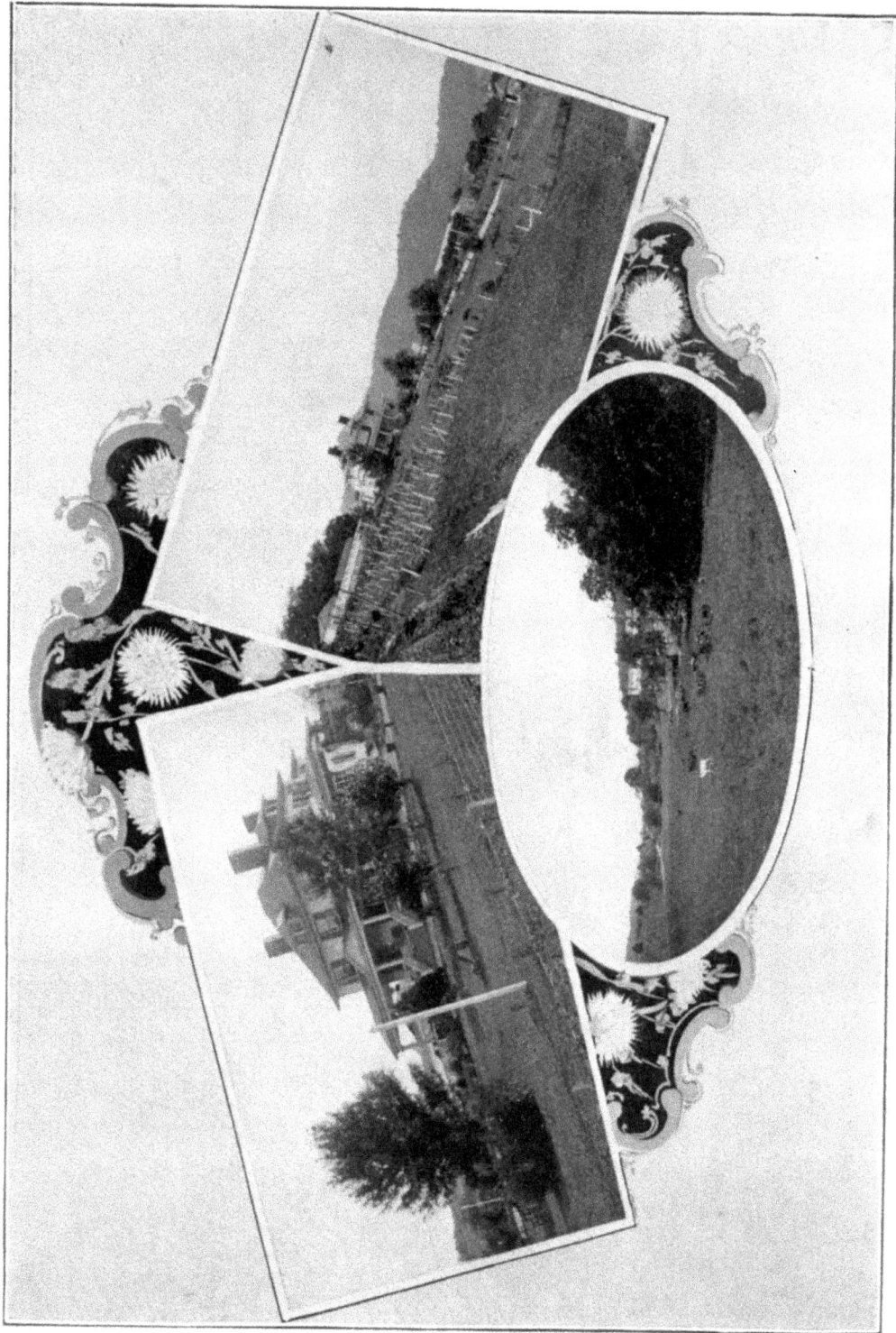

RESIDENCE, GROUNDS AND PASTURE ON FARM OF MR. GEORGE W. CALLAHAN AT DANTE,
FIVE MILES NORTH OF KNOXVILLE.

SECTIONAL VIEW OF "IDLEHOUR," THE 1200-ACRE ESTATE OF MR. JAMES P. McDONALD, FOUR MILES EAST OF KNOXVILLE.

"IDLEHOUR," RESIDENCE OF MR. JAMES P. McDONALD, ON HIS 1200-ACRE ESTATE, FOUR MILES EAST OF KNOXVILLE.

SCENES AT "IDLEHOUR," THE 1200-ACRE FANCY STOCK FARM OF MR. JAMES P. McDONALD, FOUR MILES EAST OF KNOXVILLE.

Thoroughbred Durham and other fancy cattle. Herd of sheep, imported in 1902 from the Imperial herds of His Majesty the King of England. Herd of young mules.

"PINE CREST", RESIDENCE OF MR. WM. T. LANG, AGENT OF THE BROOKSIDE MILLS.

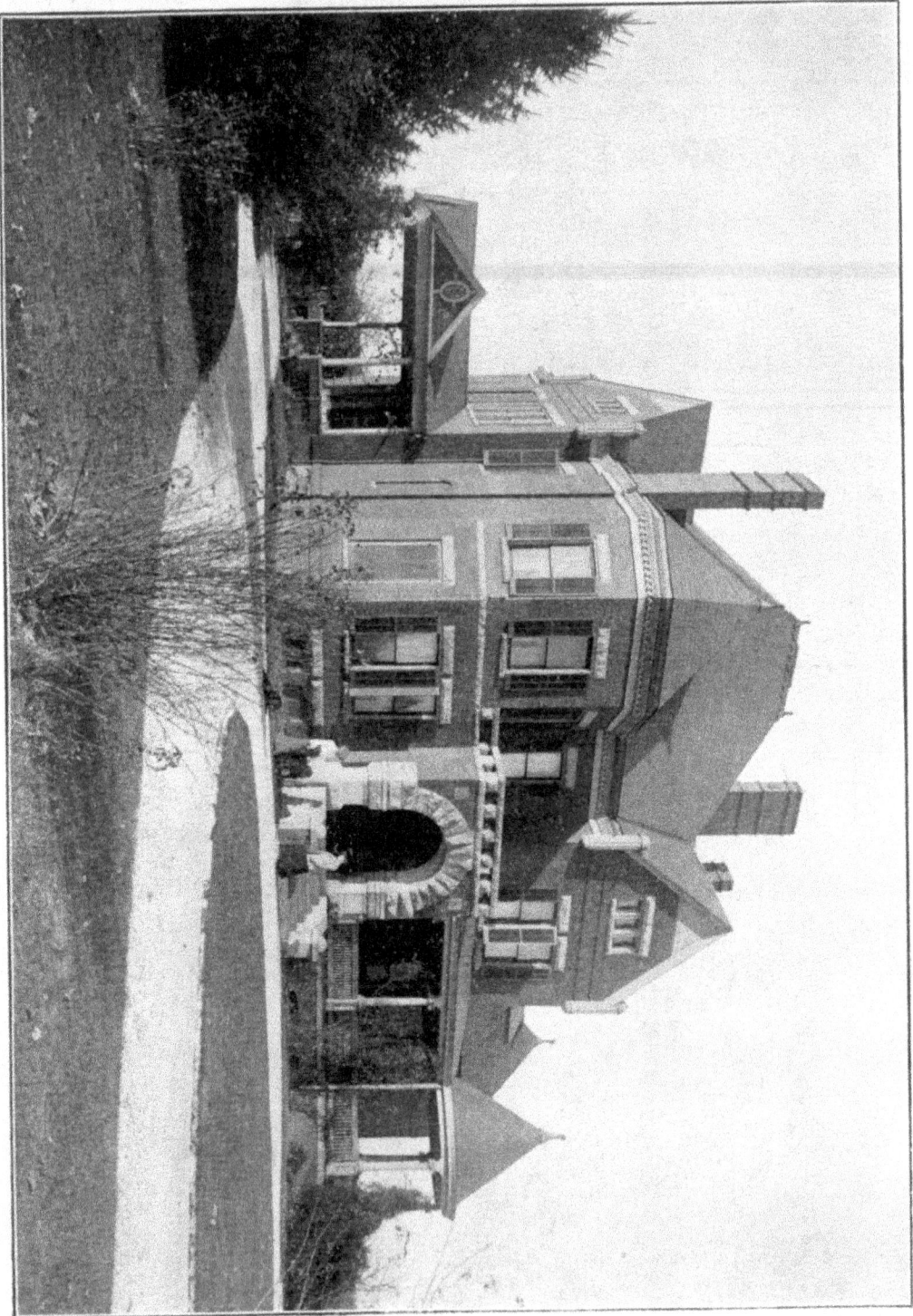

"WESTWOOD," RESIDENCE OF MR. J. E. LUTZ, KINGSTON PIKE.

"BROOKWOOD," RESIDENCE OF MR. J. C. STERCHI, MANAGER OF
THE PROCTOR FURNITURE CO., STERCHI'S ADDITION.

Barber & Kluttz, Architects, Knoxville.
RESIDENCE OF MR. S. B. NEWMAN, 422 E. SCOTT AVE.

INTERIOR OF OFFICE, HOTEL IMPERIAL.

R. W. FARR, Manager.   Rates, $2.50 to $4.50 per day.

THE CUMBERLAND.

N. M. RIDDICK, Manager.   Rates, $2.00 and $2.50 per day.
Special Weekly and Monthly Rates.

OFFICES OF DR. H. W. BROWN, SPECIALIST, 406 W. CLINCH AVE.
DR. F. H. BOMAR, ASSISTANT.

NEW MARKET HOUSE AND CITY HALL.
This is one of the finest markets in the South.

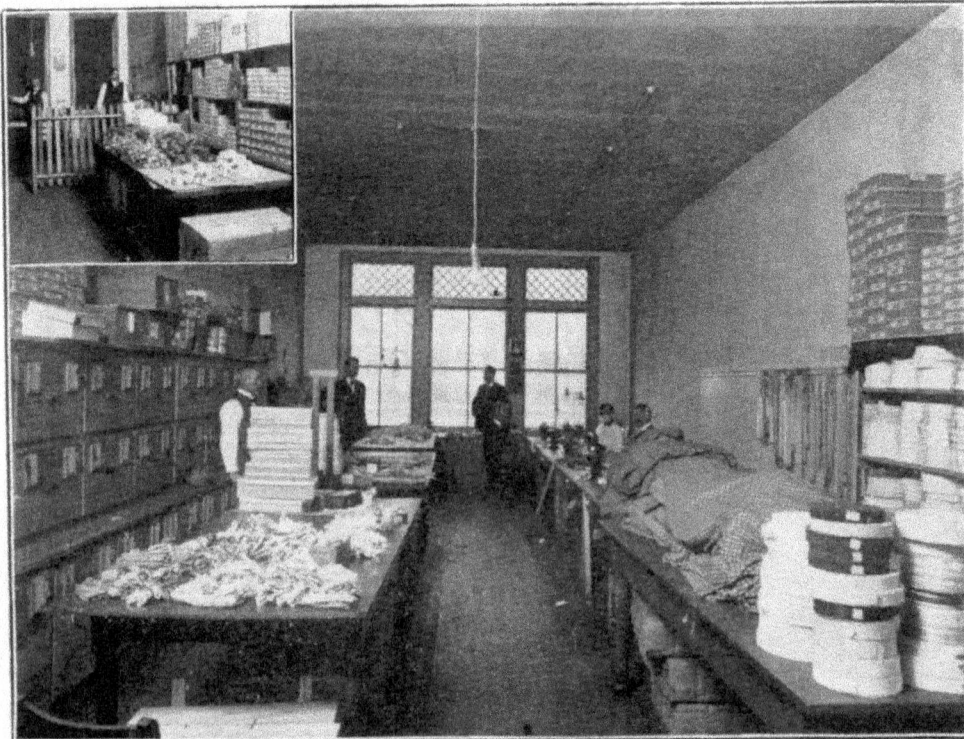

INTERIOR OF ASHMORE & HINTON, 206 VINE AVE. WEST.
Manufacturers of Suspenders and Garters.

MAIN SALESROOM GAUT-OGDEN CO.,

Stationers, Printers and Blank Book Makers. "Anything for Any Office."

EAST TENNESSEE NATIONAL BANK BUILDING.

State and U. S. Depository.   Capital Stock, $175,000.00.
          Surplus Fund and Profits (net), $241,004.50.
                    Deposits, $1,965,131.96.
F. L. FISHER, President.   W. W. WOODRUFF, Vice-President.
                    S. V. CARTER, Cashier.

DIRECTORS.

W. W. WOODRUFF,   DANIEL BRISCOE,
    Wholesale Hardware.   Wholesale Dry Goods.
C. M. McCLUNG,   L. D. TYSON,
    Wholesale Hardware.   Pres. Knoxville Cotton Mills.
PETER KERN,   JOHN McCOY,
    Wholesale Confectioner.   Real Estate.
HAL. S. HARRIS,   C. R. LOVE,
    Capitalist.   Wholesale Farm Implements.
N. W. HALE,   E. T. SANFORD,
    Wholesale Nurseries.   Lucky, Sanford & Fowler, Attys.
              F. L. FISHER, President.

Interior of
THE HOLSTON NATIONAL BANK OF KNOXVILLE.

Capital, $100,000.00.   Surplus and Profits, $17,000.

Designated United States and State Depository.

A Savings Department conducted in connection with its general banking business.

JOSEPH P. GAUT, President.   DAVID A. ROSENTHAL, Vice-President.
JNO. A. ARMSTRONG, Assistant Cashier.

DIRECTORS.

H. S. MIZNER,
        President Dixie Mills, Lenoir City, Tenn.
        Treasurer Knoxville Furniture Co., Knoxville, Tenn.

DAVID A. ROSENTHAL,
        Manufacturing and Retail Druggist.

JOHN M. ALLEN,
        Allen, Stephenson & Co.,
                Wholesale and Retail Furniture.

JNO. J. CRAIG,
        President Jno. J. Craig Marble Co.

JAMES H. COWAN,
        Claiborne, Tate & Cowan,
                Manufacturers of Clothing.

CECIL H. BAKER,
        Sec. and Treas. M. L. Ross & Co.,
                Wholesale Grocers and Candy Manufacturers.

HU. L. McCLUNG,
        Webb, McClung & Baker, Lawyers.

THOMAS R. PRICE,
        President Knoxville Furniture Co.

JOSEPH P. GAUT,
        President.

43

PETER KERN COMPANY.
Interior Retail Room and Ice Cream Parlors.

PETER KERN COMPANY.

Interior Mixing and Moulding Room, Bread Bakery. Daily capacity, 20,000 loaves bread.

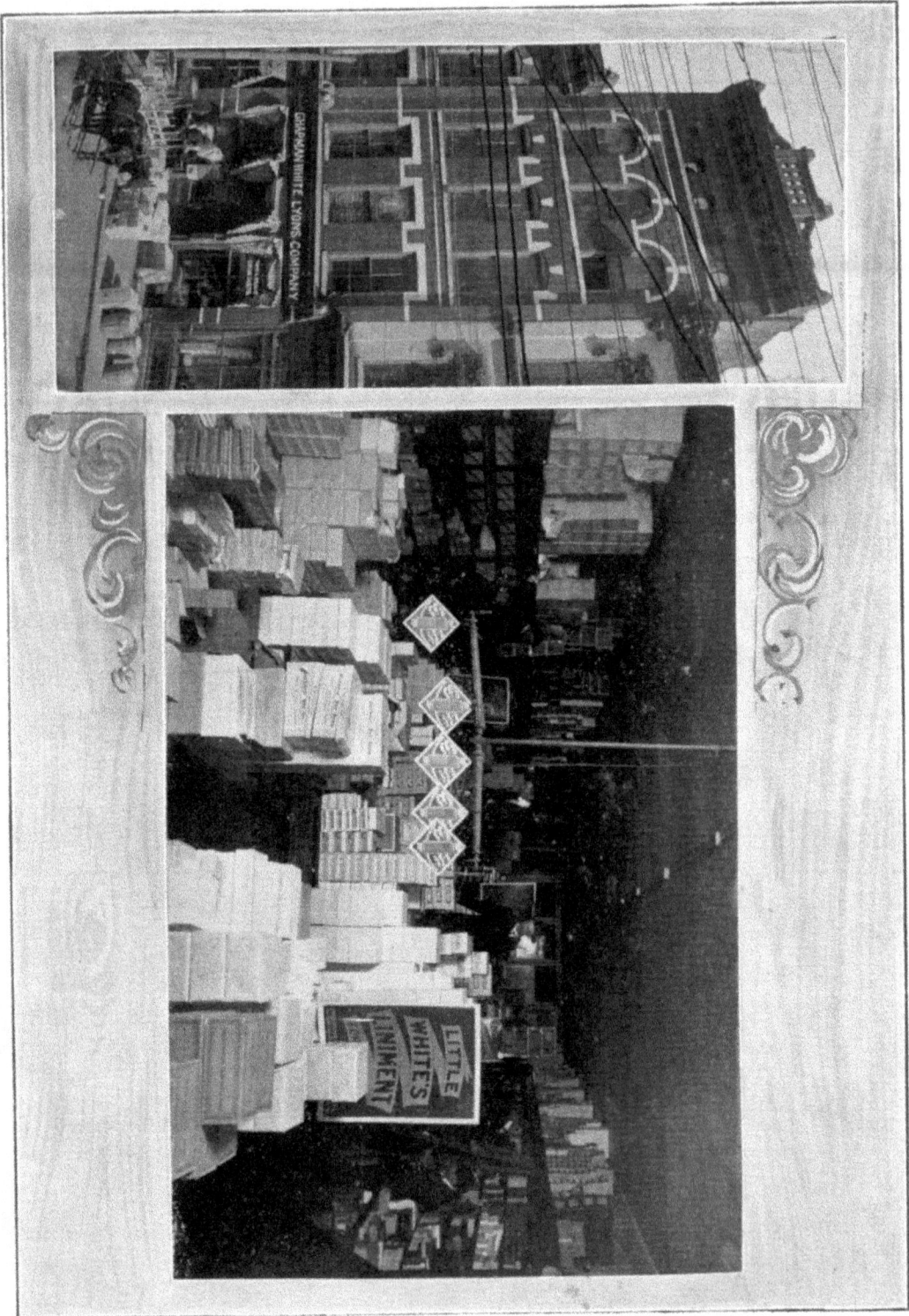

CHAPMAN, WHITE, LYONS CO. (INC.), WHOLESALE DRUGGISTS, 214 GAY STREET.
Interior Second Floor Gay Street Salesroom.
Warehouses, Jackson Avenue and Commerce Avenue.

46

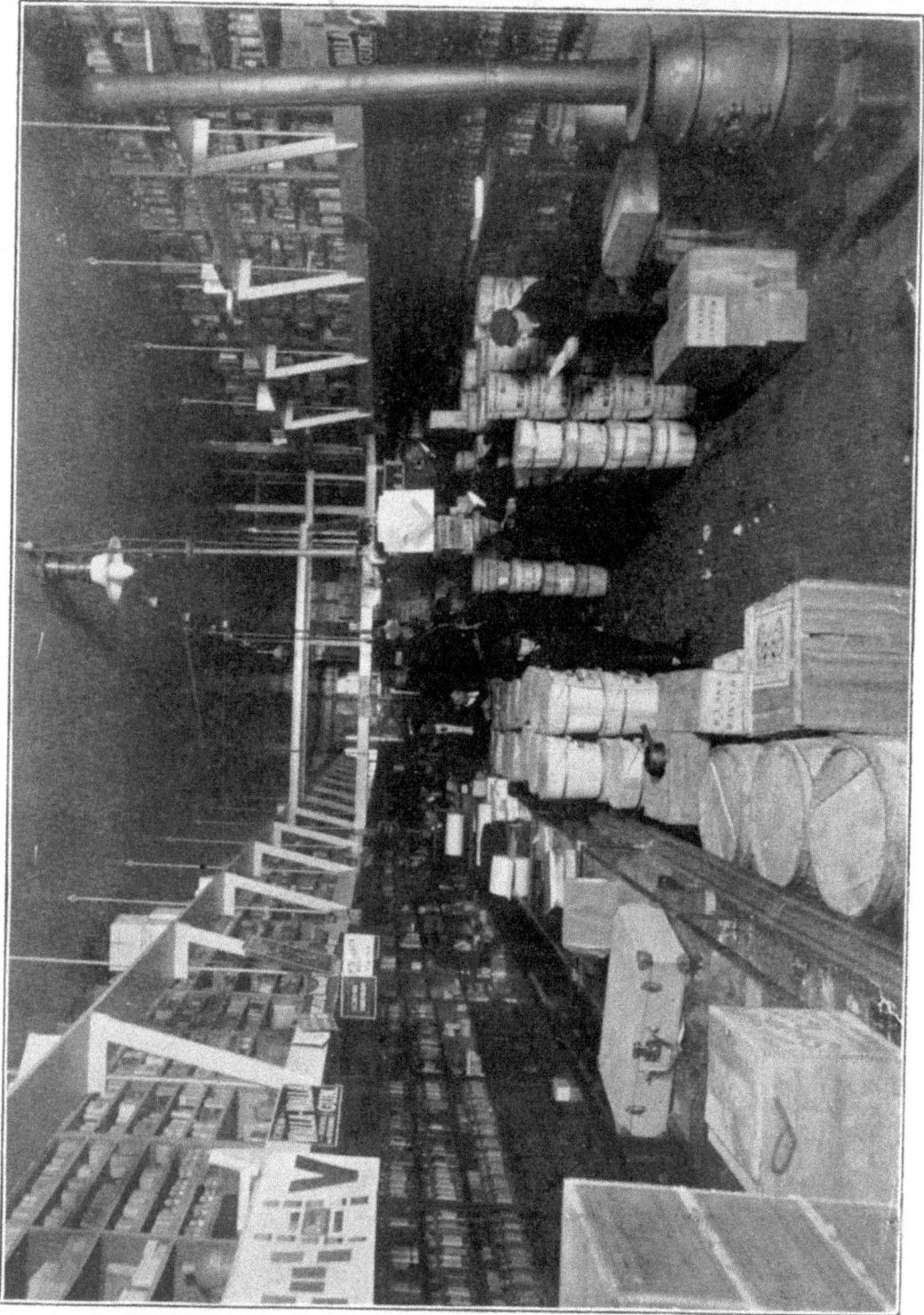

CHAPMAN. WHITE. LYONS CO. (Inc.), WHOLESALE DRUGGISTS.
Interior main salesroom, first floor, Gay St.

INTERIOR PHARMACY. F. B. SHARP.
Corner Central St. and Park Ave.

INTERIOR HOPE BROS.
Gold and Silversmiths, 519 Gay Street.

48

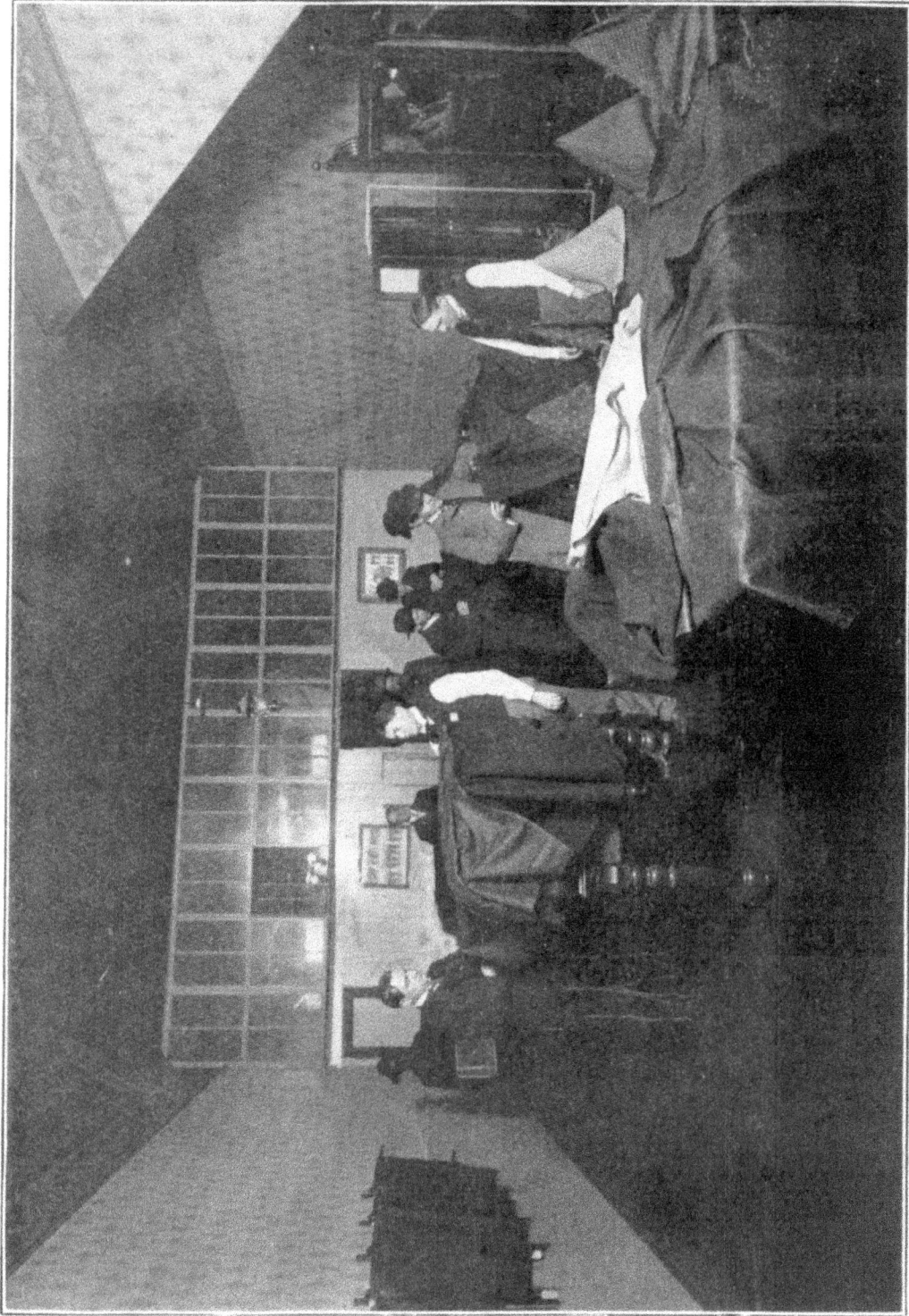

INTERIOR W. L. THOMPSON & CO., 427 GAY STREET.

Importers and Tailors.   Makers of high-class fashionable clothes.

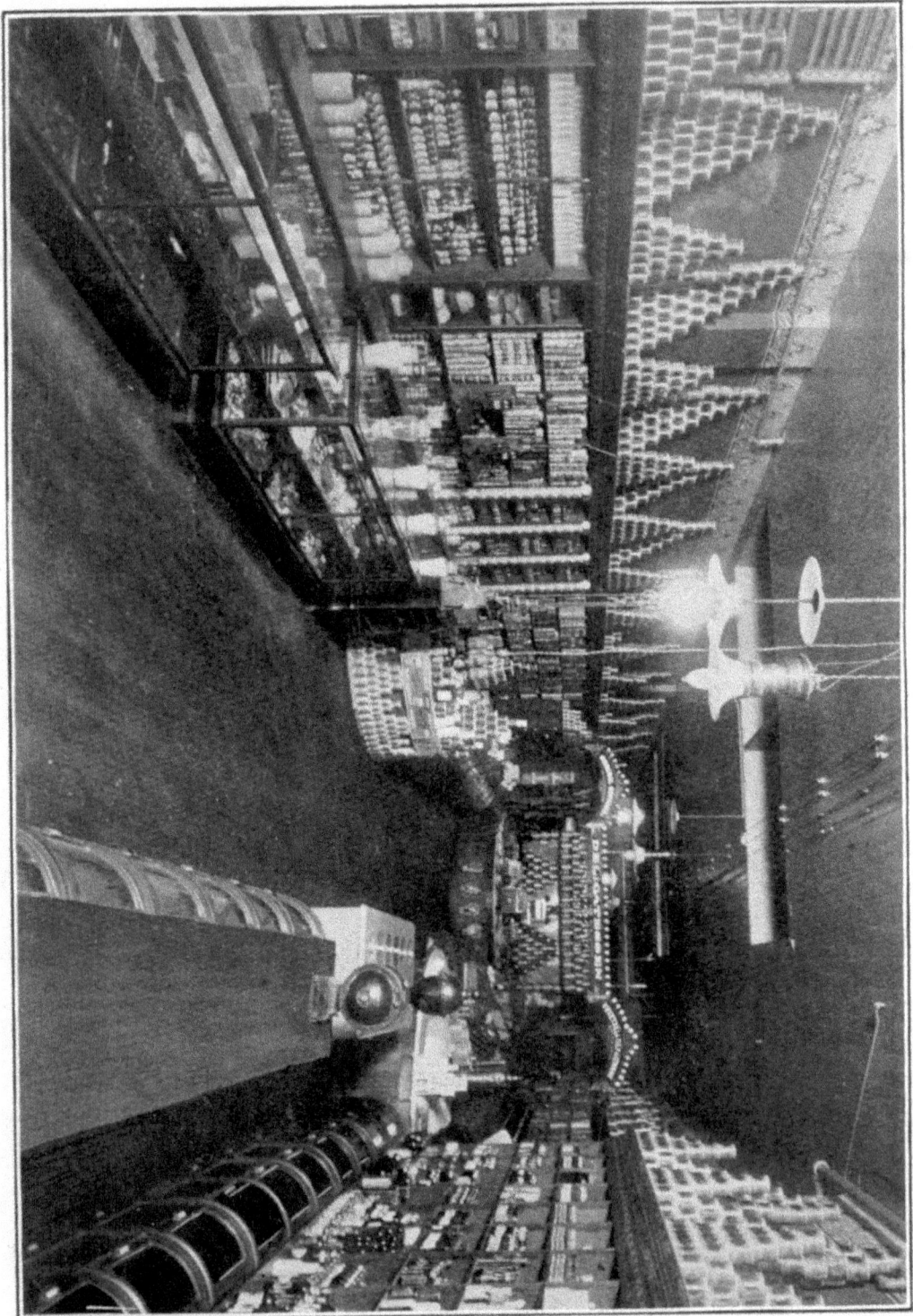

INTERIOR T. E. BURNS COMPANY (Incorporated), 319 WALL STREET
The finest grocery in the city.

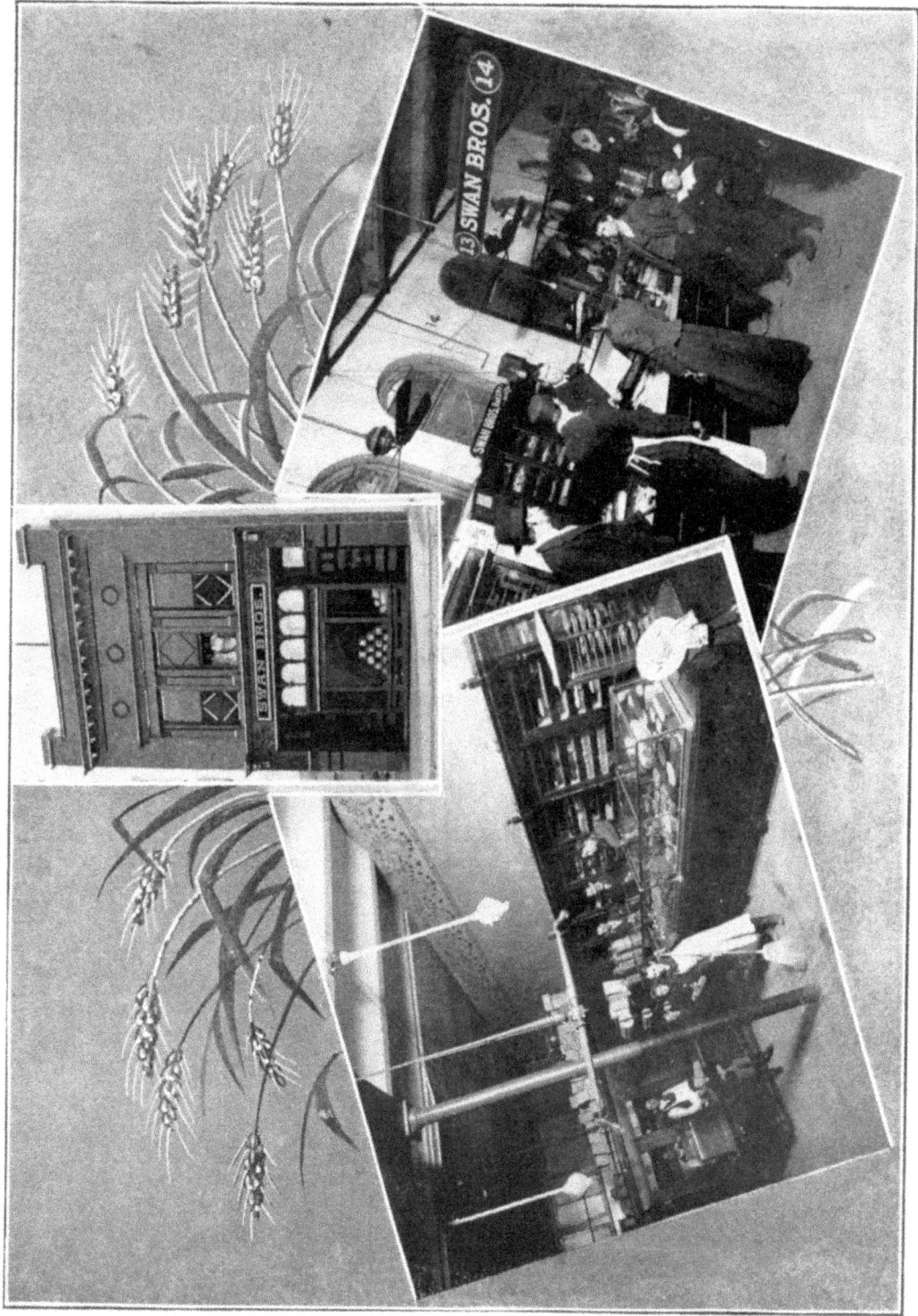

SWAN BROS.' BAKERY.

Interior Main Salesroom, 810 Central St.   Market House, Stalls Nos. 13-14.

51

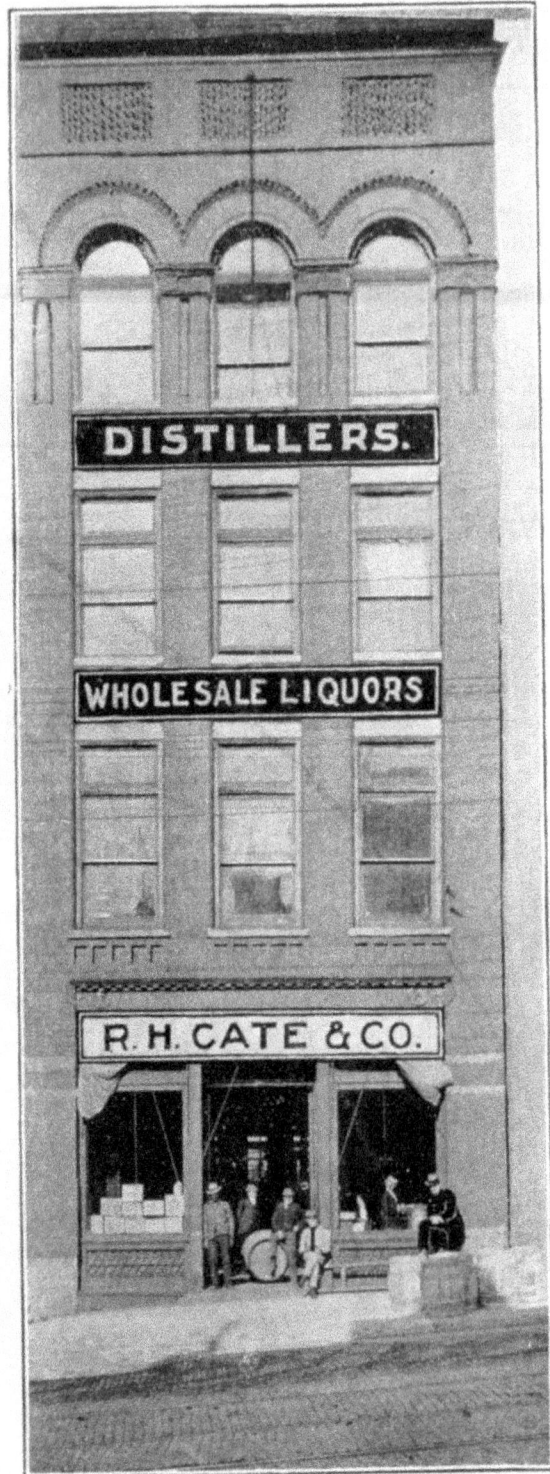

R. H. CATE & CO.,
Distillers and Wholesale Liquor Dealers.

INTERIOR KUHLMAN'S BIG CUT RATE DRUG STORE, 301 GAY ST.
Does the largest General and Prescription Business. Largest Fountain in the South.
Headquarters for all things new in Drugs and Sundries.

INTERIOR O. C. WILEY'S OPTICAL ESTABLISHMENT.
310 West Clinch Avenue.

Leon Beaver, Architect.
THE VENDOME, KNOXVILLE'S EXCLUSIVE APARTMENT HOUSE.
C. H. Paull, Manager.

BUILDING AND YARD OF CHANDLER & CO.. DEPOT AVENUE.

PLANT OF SAVAGE & TYLER.
Manufacturers of Roller Flour Mill Machinery.

BROOKSIDE MILLS

1892.

One of the largest cotton mills in the South. When completed, its equipment will consist of 90,000 spindles and 2,000 looms.

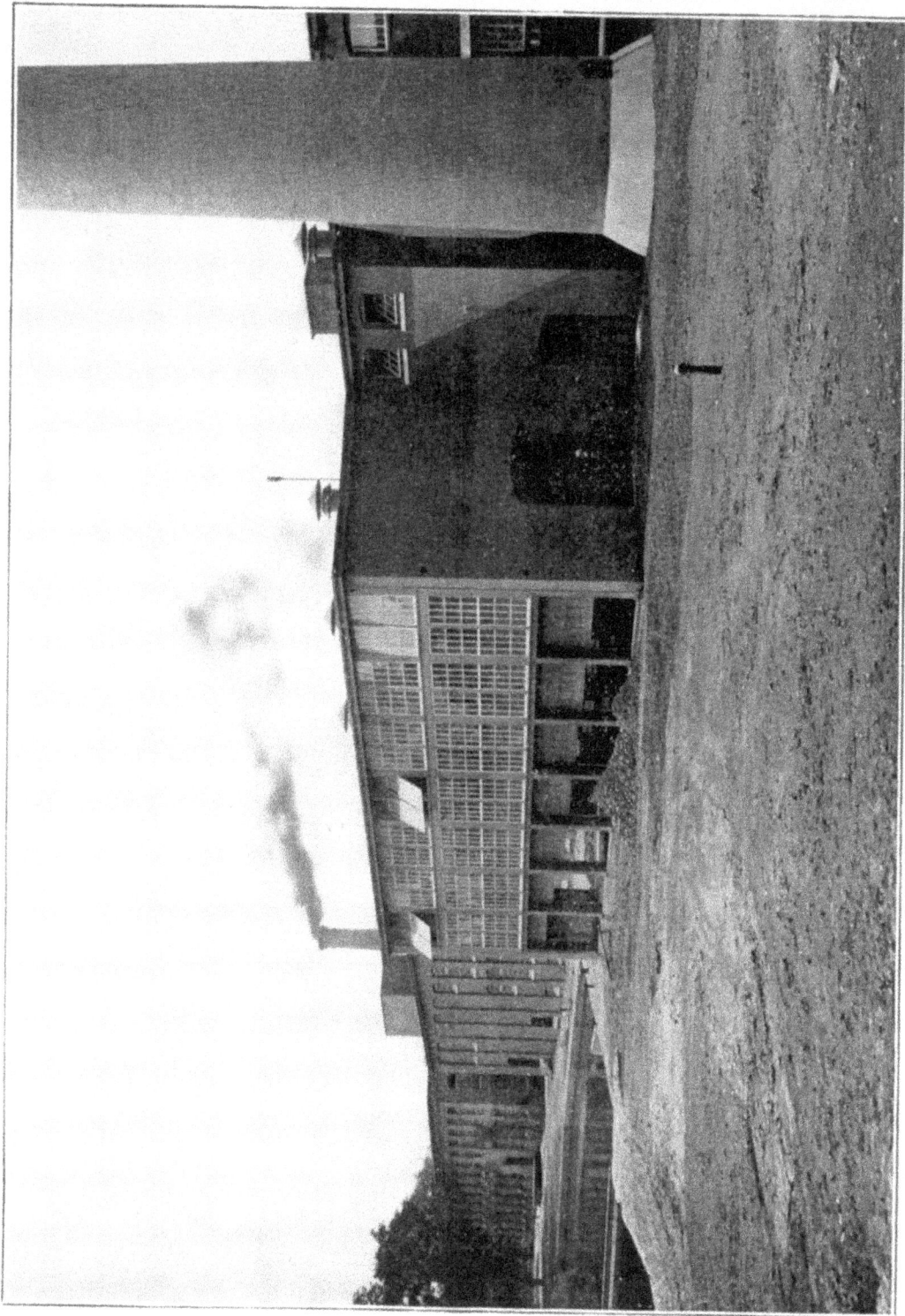

EXTERIOR BOILER HOUSE, THE BROOKSIDE MILLS.
Equipped with Continental Boilers, with Morison Corrugated Furnaces.

INTERIOR BOILER ROOM, THE BROOKSIDE MILLS.
Equipped with Continental Boilers, with Morison Corrugated Furnaces.

INTERIOR BOILER ROOM, THE BROOKSIDE MILLS.
Equipped with Continental Boilers, with Morison Corrugated Furnaces.

C. B. ATKIN'S MANTEL FACTORY, KNOXVILLE, TENN.
The output of this factory and the one on the opposite page is far in excess of any other mantel factory in the U. S.

C. B. ATKIN'S MANTEL FACTORY AT OAKWOOD.

A residential and manufacturing suburb of Knoxville, Tenn.

OAKWOOD A FOREST, JANUARY, 1902.

MORELIA AVENUE, OAKWOOD, MAY, 1902.
Showing the grading of the street and laying of the eight-inch water main.

MORELIA AVENUE, OAKWOOD, MAY, 1903.
View made from same location as ones above.

OAKWOOD, C. B. ATKIN'S ADDITION TO KNOXVILLE.
A forest in 1902. A thriving village, with 536 lots, five miles of macadamized
streets, with water mains laid in them, electric lights and
street cars, and over 100 homes in 1903.

SHOPS OF THE SOUTHERN RAILWAY, LOCATED AT LONSDALE, TWO MILES NORTH OF KNOXVILLE.

One of the largest and most complete shops of the system. Employing 1,200 men.

PLANT OF KNOXVILLE IRON COMPANY.

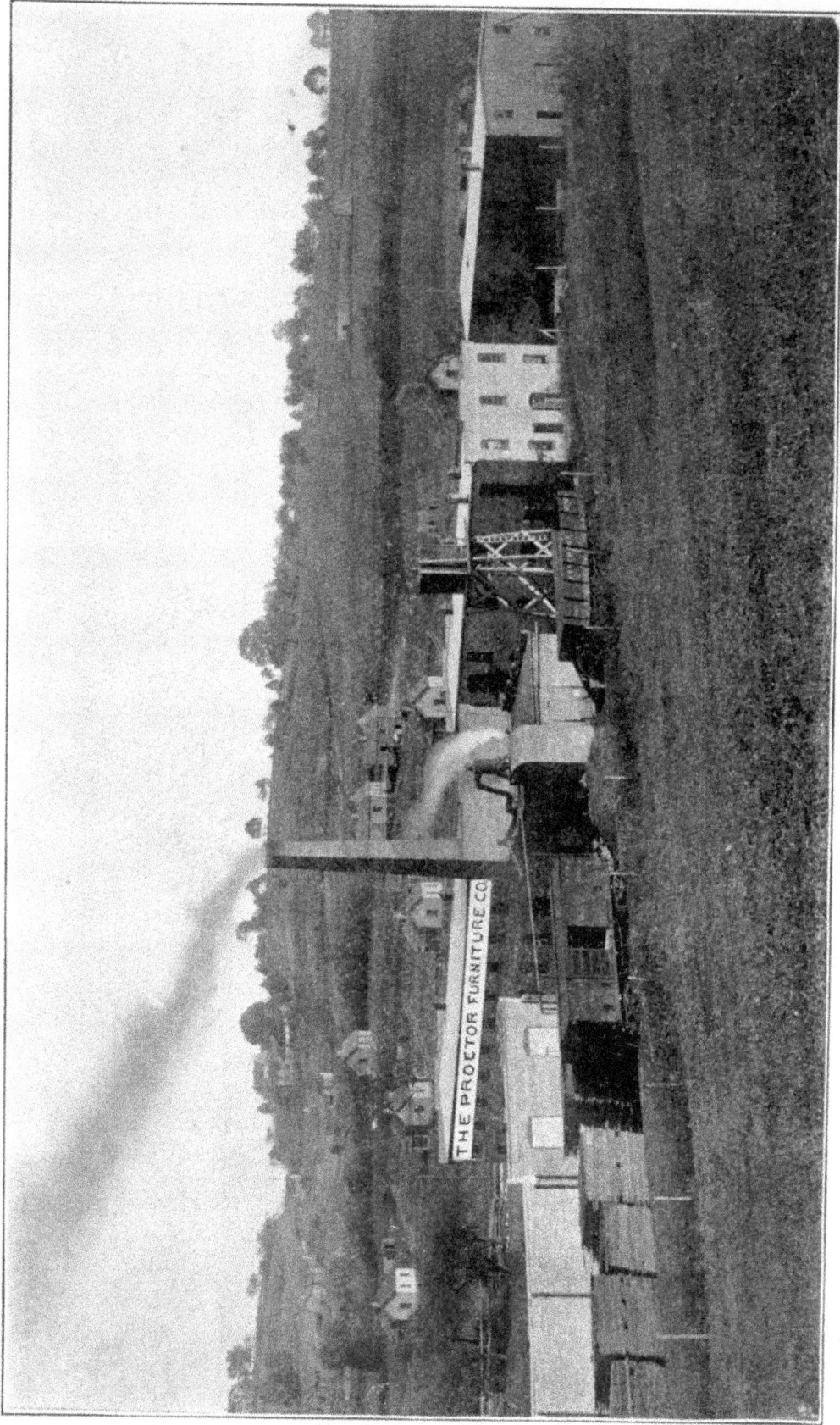

PLANT OF THE PROCTOR FURNITURE COMPANY.

Manufacturers of Bed Room Suites, Lounges, Couches and Parlor Suites. Located in Sterchi's Addition, on Lonsdale car line.

PLANT OF SOUTHERN OAK EXTRACT COMPANY.
Manufacturers of Wood and Bark Extracts.

PLANT OF COMMERCIAL MINING AND MILLING COMPANY.

Corner George Street and Southern Railway. Manufacturers of high-grade Barytes. Mines in Cocke and Monroe Counties. Office, 304 and 306 Empire Building, Knoxville, Tenn.

67

PLANT AND YARDS OF CHAVANNES LUMBER CO.

K. & O. Railway and Oldham Street. Manufacturers and Dealers in House Finishings and Lumber.

PLANT OF MURPHY & CO.

Manufacturers of Sash, Doors, Blinds, and Dealers in Lumber. Main Office and Yards, Cor. Gay Street and Front Avenue. Branch Office and Yards, Cor. Lanier and Southern Railway.

PLANT OF THE KNOXVILLE BRICK COMPANY, POWELL STATION, EIGHT MILES FROM KNOXVILLE. Manufacturers of Common Brick, and Red, Grey and Buff Pressed. Offices, 107-109 Empire Building, Knoxville.

PLANT OF THE SOUTH KNOXVILLE MACADAM COMPANY.
(Owned by Dr. T. ap R. Jones.)
Manufacturers of all kinds of Macadam and Screenings.

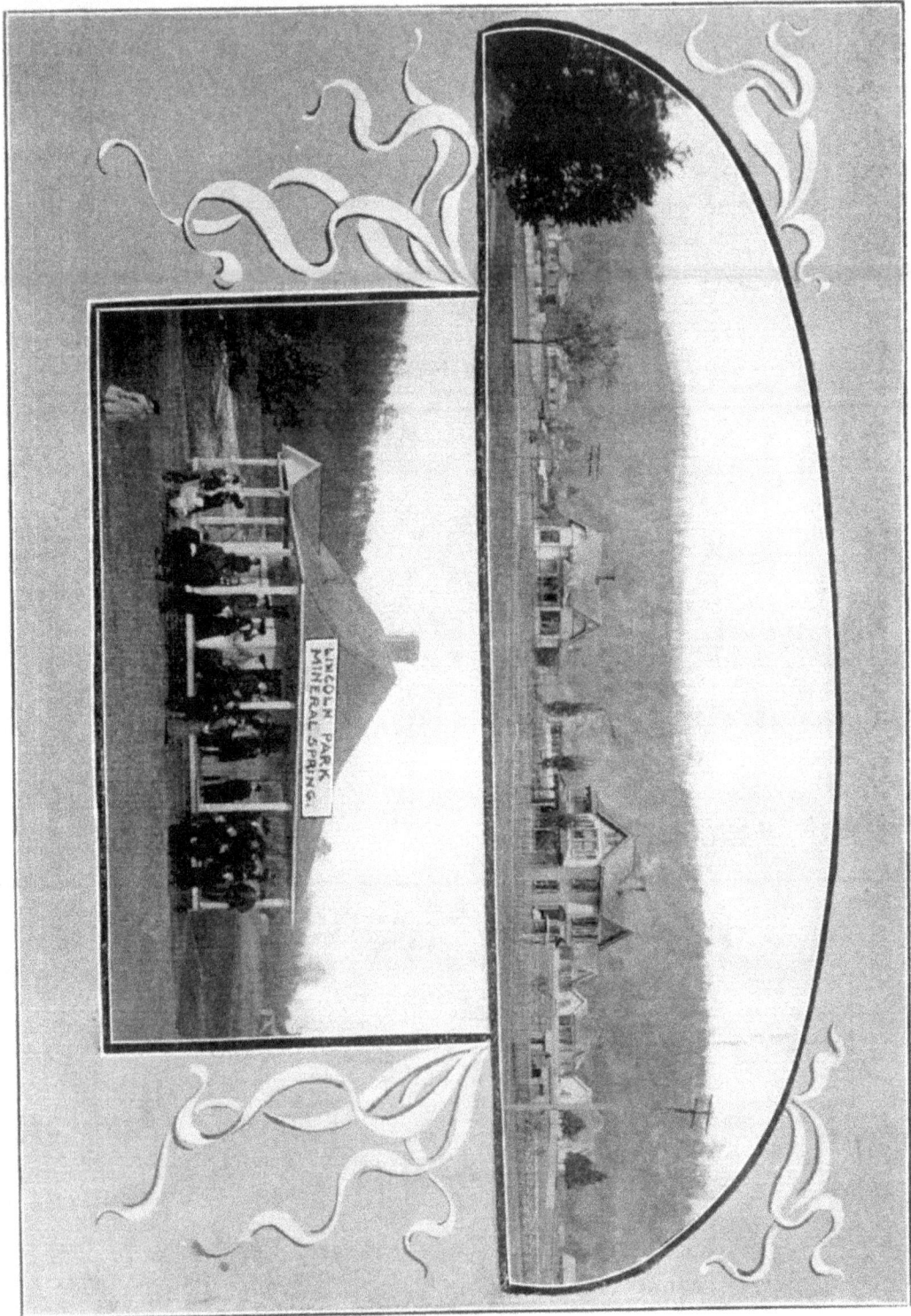

LINCOLN PARK SCENE, AND THE EPSOM, LITHIA AND CHALYBEATE MINERAL SPRINGS.

GENERAL REAL ESTATE OFFICES OF A. C. ORNDORFF AND
CITY OFFICE OF LINCOLN PARK.
611 Prince Street.

505 and 507 Jackson Avenue.

C. M. McCLUNG & CO.

Jobbers of Hardware, Mill Supplies, Stoves, Tinware. Floor space more than 100,000 square feet.

509 Jackson Avenue.

View of Sample Room.

C. M. McCLUNG & CO.

Jobbers of Hardware, Vehicles and Kindred Lines. Twice the largest hardware house in East Tennessee.

501 and 503 Jackson Avenue.

ISLAND HOME FARM, TWO MILES EAST OF KNOXVILLE, ON THE TENNESSEE RIVER.

SECTIONAL VIEW OF MECHANICSVILLE (NINTH WARD), FROM GRAND AVENUE.

SECTIONAL VIEW OF KNOXVILLE, FROM THE BLUFF SOUTH OF THE TENNESSEE RIVER.

www.ingramcontent.com/pod-product-compliance
Lightning Source LLC
Chambersburg PA
CBHW081635040426
42449CB00014B/3327